YANKEE STADIUM
The Final Game

Then and Now

Yankee Stadium changed a lot during the years following my first Opening Day. Back in '65, the 42-year-old grandstands, decked out in red, white, and blue bunting, were still supported by poles that forced scores of fans to crane their necks for a view of the entire field. Those poles were removed in the 1970s and a Diamond Vision video screen was added. Bu

OPENING DAY, 1965. YANKEE STADIUM'S 85-YEAR LIFE IS HALF OVER. MICKEY MANTLE IS BATTING. THE GLORY YEARS (1949-1964) ARE DONE. IT WILL BE 11 YEARS BEFORE THE TEAM WINS ITS NEXT TITLE.

the original structure had its own appeal: Its huge scoreboard continuously displayed the scores for all out-of-town games simultaneously. And gaps in the Stadium's outer wall provided a nice view of the playing field from the 161st Street subway platform. The Yankees lost that 1965 opener, 7-2, although Mickey Mantle did hit the 457th home run of his career.

CLOSING DAY, 2008. YANKEE STADIUM'S 85-YEAR LIFE IS NEARLY OVER. THE YANKEES ARE ON THE VERGE OF ELIMINATION FROM THE PENNANT RACE. ANOTHER STRING OF GLORY YEARS (1995-2007) HAS ENDED.

For Hannah, without whose love and support this book
would not have been possible.

Yankee Stadium: The Final Game
A Fan Says Good-bye
www.YankeeStadiumTheFinalGame.com

For information about a printed copy of any image
in this book, e-mail: print@veridico.com

Published by Veridico Publishing LLC
P.O. Box 1006
Paramus, New Jersey 07653
www.Veridico.com

Cover design by Jeff Fox
Interior design by Tim LaPalme

ISBN-10: 0-9823656-0-8
ISBN-13: 978-0-9823656-0-1

Library of Congress Control Number: 2009923974

Printed in the United States of America

My Love Affair with Yankee Stadium

I was born in the Bronx, but until May 26, 1962, I'd only seen Yankee Stadium in the grays of a black-and-white TV. At 11 years old, my first real glimpse of it came as a shock: Oxidized by 39 years of exposure to the elements, the Stadium's copper green facade stared at me above the jumble of the surrounding neighborhood.

Soon I witnessed something even more dramatic: A sparkling emerald infield, no longer just a blob of gray on a TV screen, rising into view as my father and I strode up the runway to our ground-level, $2.50 seats on the first base side. (A pole blocked my view of first base). The game itself was memorable: Detroit Tiger star outfielder Al Kaline broke his collarbone trying to make a difficult catch.

During the 46 years that followed, a period representing about half the Stadium's lifetime and most of mine, I'd spend many memorable hours in what legendary sportscaster Art Rust, Jr., called "the big ball orchard in the Bronx."

Some of the events I witnessed:

Old Timers Day 1963, 15 World Series games, dozens of playoff games, four Opening Days, Mickey Mantle Day 1965, Bat Day 1965, "Jeffrey Maier" game 1996, First Yankee/Met game 1997, AL pennant-clinching 1998, Tino's Series slam 1998, World Series clinching 1999, Subway Series 2000, Clemens/Piazza thrown bat, first game after 9/11, back-to-back 2001 World Series miracle comebacks, Giambi walk-off grand slam game 2002, Aaron Boone walk-off pennant-clincher 2003, and ALCS game 7 in 2004.

I remember walking along E. 157 St. in the early '60s, when it was still a street, not a pedestrian mall with fenced-in picnic tables.

Then there was the time a female fan ran topless in the stands (a sportswriter wrote, "there were two out in the ninth"); and another when a fan fell from the upper deck (he was unhurt, but arrested); and yet another when a fan raced across the outfield to greet Bernie Williams (the fan was arrested).

I witnessed Yankee coach Don Zimmer get hit in the head in the dugout by a Chuck Knoblauch foul ball. And

BEFORE TICKETMASTER. TO BUY THIS TICKET, I WAITED ON LINE OUTSIDE THE STADIUM FOR SEVERAL HOURS THE MORNING OF 1963 WORLD SERIES GAME 2.

Armando Benitez set off a fistfight in '98 by plunking Tino Martinez in the back.

I've banged Freddie Sez's frying pan with his spoon. And outlasted two-hour rain delays.

I've run around the Stadium's diamond as an adult (during the off-season), pretending to be my childhood hero, Mickey Mantle.

I've sat in nosebleed grandstand seats, the far reaches of the left-center field bleachers, and the first box behind the Yankee dugout. I've seen mounds of snow on the sidelines in April and shivered through the first major league game ever played in the month of November.

I've staggered along River Avenue in a state of delirium at a World Series Championship, then again too soon in shock at a four-game collapse at the hands of the hated Red Sox.

All of which gave me a lot of memories to reflect on when I set off for my final visit on September 21, 2008.

One thing I knew: Watching the game itself wouldn't be enough. Especially since the Yankees were about to be eliminated from the post-season for the first time in 15 years.

No. I needed to soak up the neighborhood in all its glory and filth, observing it as it would never quite be again.

One final time, I'd elbow my way through the crowd on the sidewalk in front of Stan the Man's Baseball Land. And watch the bleacher creatures file into their section of the ballpark.

If radio announcements that weekend were to be believed, arriving early would afford me the privilege of one final stroll on the field, accompanied, of course, by Aura and Mystique.

By the time I arrived, it was a warm, Sunday autumn afternoon.

As with so many of my previous Stadium outings over the years, I left home intent on capturing every aspect of the experience with my camera. And, this time, also with my words.

One of my earliest Stadium photos (the shot of Opening Day, 1965, on page 2), was captured with my trusty Kodak Brownie.

Even if the Yankee management wasn't going to cooperate (as it turned out, many earlycomers weren't permitted on the field), the weather would.

And so I began my last visit by walking down the center of River Avenue...

Jeff Fox
April 2009

One Last Time: The Chronology

The Neighborhood

The El rumbles overhead, as always. Hot dog vendors set up as usual. But something's different. River Avenue seems emptier and more people than usual are taking photos.

Maybe they think these souvenir stands won't be here next year. The stores probably will, but for the first time in 85 years, most won't be directly opposite the ballpark. The new Yankee Stadium is nearing completion farther down River Avenue, on the left in this photo (but beyond camera range).

The sidewalks on both sides of River Avenue are packed, prime territory for scalpers and pickpockets (next page). Still, not everyone on the street today is awed by the occasion's significance (page 11).

On the sidewalk outside left field, pitcher Joba Chamberlain's wheelchair-bound father, Harlan, patiently signs autographs for the public (page 14).

Although the crowd around him grows, there seems to be no security detail. Undaunted, he basks in his son's glory.

TICK TOCK. THROUGHOUT THIS BOOK I'VE ADDED CLOCKS TO NOTE THE TIME EVENTS OCCURRED.

< THE
SIDEWALKS OF
NEW YORK.
RIVER AVENUE
IS MY YELLOW
BRICK ROAD
TO THE POTATO
KNISHES AND
MATZOH-BALL
SOUP YOU CAN
ONLY GET AT
THE COURT
DELI ON 161ST
STREET.

< A FAN'S LOVE. WHAT GREATER DEVOTION CAN THERE BE THAN WRAPPING YOURSELF IN OLD GLORY AND SPORTING LAST NEW YEAR'S EVE'S GLASSES?

11

BLEACHER ENTRY

12

< JUST AS THEY WERE THEN. MEMORIES FLOODED BACK OF PASSING THROUGH THESE TURNSTILES, ARMED WITH A DIRT-CHEAP BLEACHER TICKET, MY LITTLE LEAGUE GLOVE, AND HOPE.

PROUD DAD. HARLAN CHAMBERLAIN, JOBA'S FATHER, SIGNS AUTOGRAPHS OUTSIDE THE STADIUM.

14

Early Arrivals

They had told us that if we arrived early enough, say at 1 or 2, we'd get to walk on the field. That's not how it worked out. When I arrived, there were no signs directing us to the field, nor anyone to answer our questions.

Eventually, thousands of us massed under the left field stands, near the entrance to Monument Park.

We remained there for about an hour, unwilling to give up our last chance to tread on hallowed ground. It was stifling. Someone fainted near a lemonade stand.

Finally, they let us into the Stadium, but not on the field.

Thousands of others did make it onto the field (page 17), but we were diverted to Monument Park (page 18).

We settled for snapshots of the grounds crew making its last pre-game run (page 20). As I made my way back toward the infield, A-Rod approached us in the left field corner, surrounded by security guards. He mugged for us (page 22), high-fived a fan, then disappeared whence he came. After that, we waited hours (page 23) for something of importance to happen.

AT LAST!
AFTER WE'D
SPENT MORE
THAN AN
HOUR PENNED
BENEATH
THE STANDS,
THE SUN AND
LEFT-FIELD
GRASS WERE
WELCOME
SIGHTS.

17

< AWESOME!
THE SHEER
LENGTH OF
MONUMENT PARK
DROVE HOME
JUST HOW MANY
UNFORGETTABLE
YANKEES HAD
SWATTED,
FLUNG, AND
SPRINTED THEIR
WAY ABOUT THE
SURROUNDING
10 ACRES.

< FINAL RUN.
EVEN
SOMETHING AS
MUNDANE AS
THE GROUNDS
CREW TOOK ON
POIGNANCY:
I WAS
WITNESSING
THE VERY
LAST OF THEIR
THOUSANDS
UPON
THOUSANDS
OF APPOINTED
ROUNDS.

21

< **CAMEO.** THE
AFTERNOON'S
MONOTONY
IS BRIEFLY
INTERRUPTED
WHEN A-ROD
STROLLS OUT
FOR A VISIT AND
SOME PHOTO
OPS. AFTER
THAT, IT'S BACK
TO THE LONG
WAIT.

23

Batting Practice

The media circus around the batting cage is like that of a World Series game, with everybody interviewing everybody.

Some fans find a nice perch from which to watch the Oriole hitters (page 31). The orange-and-black clad Birds are props, overlooked but essential to this celebration cum memorial service.

Panning around the Stadium, I spot the Bleacher Creatures (page 32) and the nose-bleed section in the right field upper deck (page 33), just below where Mickey Mantle's 1963 blast off the original Stadium's facade came closer to being the only fair ball hit out of this park than any in history.

The two foul poles (page 37) stand as the goal posts between which all home runs in the history of Yankee Stadium have had to pass. As the autumn sun sets behind packed stands for the very last time (page 38), the scene it evokes could easily be from any night game in the past few decades.

26

314 FT.

SHOWTIME.
SCADS OF
REPORTERS.
JOHN STERLING
HOLDING COURT
IN A DIRECTOR'S
CHAIR.
WELCOME TO
THIS THEATER'S
FINAL
PERFORMANCE
OF THAT LONG-
RUNNING SHOW,
THE BRONX
ZOO.

29

< **VANTAGE POINT.** ONE OF THE TREATS IN SITTING THIS FAR FROM THE FIELD IS GETTING TO WATCH THE PEOPLE IN THE PRICEY FIELD BOXES SCURRY FOR COVER WHEN IT RAINS.

< **Far reaches.**
This is the
section of the
Stadium that
puts Yankee
players
through a
first-inning
roll call,
chanting
each player's
name until
he turns and
waves. My
favorite ever:
Ber-nie
Will-iams!

35

< THE END IS NEAR. AMIDST ALL THE POMP, A STARK REMINDER.

One Last Time

If there's a common thought in the heads of practically everyone here, it's that every sight they see today they will be seeing for the last time. See it now, do it now, capture it now...or forever hold your peace.

At right, Jorge Posada takes advantage of his injured status to grab some fleeting digital photos of the original monuments before they're uprooted and transported across the street to their new home.

Then there are the final visits to the food courts (next page). Much of the Stadium's life takes place down here beneath the grandstand, out of view of the players and TV cameras.

This is where we huddle when our

seats are too cold or damp. And where we come to fill our bellies, even if the fare is usually overpriced, and sometimes barely edible. Would you trust sushi from the section 18 food court (page 42)? And why are those little ice cream balls the "ice cream of the future"? Is regular ice cream dying?

When life deals you a lemon, squeeze its juice into a cup (page 43).

< **HANGOUT.**
I'VE WATCHED
AN INNING
AND A HALF ON
THIS TV WHILE
WAITING ON
LINE FOR FOOD
HERE.

42

Lemonade
$5.00

Cotton
Candy
$4.00

43

Ceremony

Baseball is nothing, if not ceremony: There's the national anthem, seventh inning stretch, and Hall of Fame induction.

Tonight's event offers lots of ceremonies. In the photo at right, the Yankees' first pennant, from 1922, is displayed.

Most of the ceremonies involve Yankee greats, living or dead. Actors portray Ruth, Gehrig, and other ancients (page 47).

Some retired stars are introduced live, position by position (pages 48 thru 56). A few active players join them on the field. When have so many Yankee heroes taken the field together? Maybe never.

Some deceased stars (Howard, Hunter, Mantle, Maris, Martin, Munson, and Riz-

zuto) are represented by family members.

Some living stars are absent: Joe Torre and Don Mattingly, both currently exiled to Dodger Stadium. Roger Clemens. And what about Cy Young reliever Sparky

Lyle? Not to worry. Most will return someday.

Many other Yankees who aren't here tonight are acknowledged by name and face on the video scoreboard in right field.

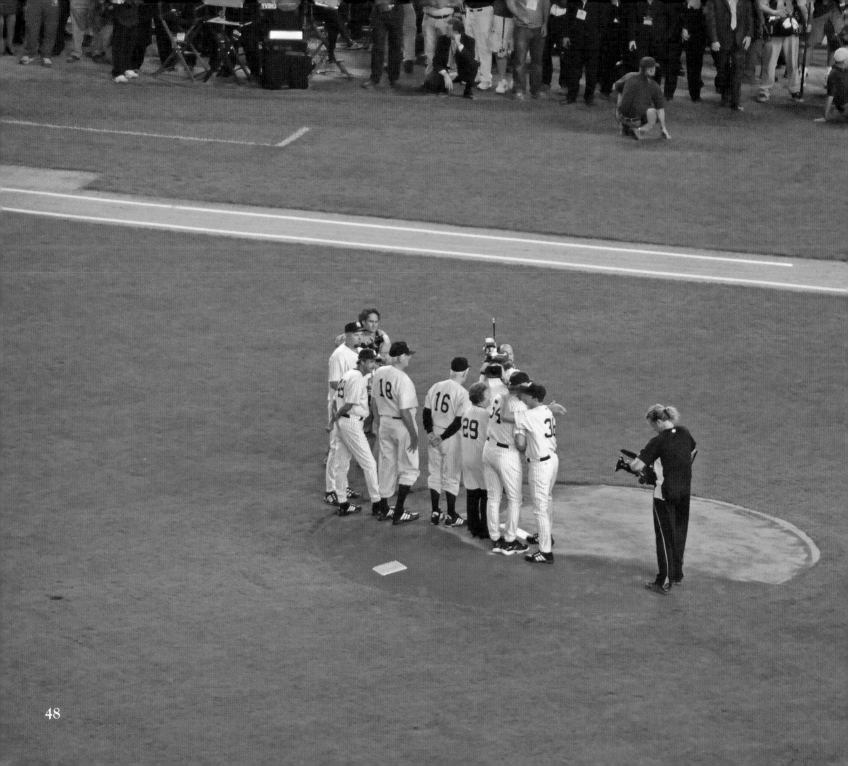

> LEFT FIELD.
(LEFT TO
RIGHT) HIDECKI
MATSUI, REGGIE
JACKSON, DAVE
WINFIELD, AND
JORGE POSADA.

> ON THE
MOUND. (LEFT
TO RIGHT)
DAVID WELLS,
RON GUIDRY,
DON LARSEN,
WHITEY
FORD, HELEN
HUNTER,
GOOSE
GOSSAGE, AND
DAVID CONE.

49

< IN CENTER. BERNIE WILLIAMS' FIRST APPEARANCE AT THE STADIUM SINCE RETIREMENT. JOINING HIM ARE DAVID MANTLE AND THE FAMILY OF BOBBY MURCER.

< IN RIGHT. PAUL O'NEILL ACKNOWLEDGES THE CROWD. JOINING HIM ARE ROY WHITE AND RANDY MARIS.

50

> HOT CORNER.
SCOTT BROSIUS,
WADE BOGGS,
AND GRAIG
NETTLES.

< SHORTSTOP.
DEREK
JETER, CORA
RIZZUTO (WITH
MARIANO
RIVERA), AND
GENE (STICK)
MICHAEL.

> **AT SECOND.**
WILLIE
RANDOLPH
SLIDES ONE
LAST TIME.

> (LEFT
TO RIGHT)
ROBINSON
CANO, WILLIE
RANDOLPH,
BOBBY
RICHARDSON,
AND BILLY
MARTIN JR.

53

< AT FIRST.
BILL (MOOSE)
SKOWRON,
CHRIS
CHAMBLISS,
TINO
MARTINEZ, AND
JASON GIAMBI.

< BEHIND
THE PLATE.
MICHAEL
MUNSON,
YOGI BERRA,
AND CHERYL
HOWARD.

THE HOUSE THAT RUTH CLOSED. BABE RUTH'S 92-YEAR-OLD DAUGHTER, JULIA STEVENS RUTH, TAKES THE FIELD. . .

. . .AND TOSSES THE CEREMONIAL FIRST PITCH. . .

IT'S LOW!

57

Play Ball!

Oh yeah, there's also a game to play to-night. Not that anyone much cares. After five years of decline, the Yankees are headed for elimination from post-season play for the first time since 1993. If they win tonight (and they did), they'll merely postpone the inevitable for a day.

In the photo at right, Pettitte's first pitch is greeted by camera flashes throughout the Stadium.

The game's most intriguing questions: Will the Yankees end the Stadium's run on a winning note? Who will be the last pitcher and hitter? Who will hit the last home run? Every inning is laden with answers to future trivia questions.

Damon's home run (next page) looks like it might be the Stadium's last. But then Jose Molina hits one and joins the Babe (who hit the first) in the Yankee record books. Grabbed by a Wyoming official (page 61), the ball's ownership is later disputed.

Other highlights: A message from 98-year-old Stadium PA announcer, Bob Sheppard (page 64); Pettitte's final curtain call (page 65); Rivera's final entrance (page 66); and the final out (page 67).

> **THE FINAL HOME RUN.** WHO'D HAVE THOUGHT THE HONOR WOULD FOREVER BELONG TO BACKUP CATCHER JOSE MOLINA, WHO HIT JUST THREE HOME RUNS ALL SEASON? ANOTHER ODDITY: THE FAN IN THE WHITE HAT AND BLUE JERSEY COULDN'T WRESTLE THE HISTORIC BALL THROUGH THE NET, BUT DID EVENTUALLY TAKE POSSESSION.

GETTING IT GOING. JOHNNY DAMON'S THIRD INNING BLAST PUT THE YANKEES AHEAD TO STAY.

 SALUTING THE FINAL SEASON AT YANKEE STADIUM

TONIGHT'S ATTENDANCE IS THE TOTAL ATTENDANCE IN THE 85 YEAR HISTORY OF YANKEE STADIUM:

151,959,005

THANK YOU TO THE BEST BASEBALL FANS IN THE WORLD!!!

metlife.

REGULAR SEASON CO

MetLife   Foreve

< THE VOICE OF YANKEE STADIUM. NOT WELL ENOUGH TO ATTEND, BOB SHEPPARD SENT A VIDEO SALUTE. HOW FITTING THAT THE ONLY STADIUM VOICE MOST OF US HAVE EVER KNOWN, THE SAME VOICE THAT ECHOED ACROSS THESE STANDS BACK WHEN DIMAGGIO AND MANTLE PATROLLED THIS OUTFIELD TOGETHER, SHOULD ECHO HERE AGAIN AS THE FINAL CURTAIN DESCENDED.

DIAMOND VISION

399FT.

> FINAL OUT.
THIS IS WHAT
IT LOOKED LIKE
THE MOMENT
THEY STOPPED
PLAYING
BASEBALL
IN YANKEE
STADIUM
FOREVER.

ENTER SANDMAN.
RIVERA TREKS IN
FOR THE LAST TIME.

End Game

As the voice of the Yankees, John Sterling, might put it: "Ballgame over. Yankee Stadium over." In the photo at right, Sterling is immortalized by having his face and trademark call ("the-e-e Yankees win-n-n") flashed on the scoreboard.

Players whoop it up (next page). This will be the last time this year they'll get to celebrate this much.

Then, Yankee captain Derek Jeter gives a heartfelt speech about tradition and continuity. He leads teammates around the field in a salute to fans (pages 70 and 71).

There are some final photos on the mound (page 72) as the media swarm in.

Mounted police straddle the foul lines

(page 73) to keep overzealous fans from storming their heroes. (Chris Chambliss' pennant-clinching HR, anyone?)

Then the team and family members get to play on the turf (page 74). Club officials and their guests scoop up souvenir

infield dirt, as Yankees' General Manager Brian Cashman looks on (page 75).

Many of us linger, reluctant to say goodbye. Some reportedly remain until the wee hours.

71

> SEIZE THE
TIME. AND
SOME OF THE
INFIELD DIRT.

Final Exit

So that's it. The witching hour. Time to trudge down those ramps, tossing familiar sights a final glance. It seems just plain unreal that this walk will be our last. Surely next week or next month, we'll make this trek again.

Memories rush back of fans who'd had one beer too many storming down the ramps, chanting "Yankees win" or "Boston sucks." Or, following crushing defeats, of grim silence punctuated by a taunt or two from a fan of the opposition.

Will the new Yankee Stadium have similar ramps, or has modern architecture come up with a better way to get around? Tune in next year.

Surely the new Stadium will be cleaner

and spiffier, with wireless Internet, food kiosks, and programmed high-def video displays. But will it have Aura and Mystique? Or will we have to create those vibes all over again?

All day, I'd wanted to capture both of the Yankee Stadiums in a single scene, but hadn't found a meaningful shot. Then, as I exited, old and new combined to offer the elegant solution on page 79: "Crossing the threshold."

> CROSSING THE THRESHOLD. BEHIND US LAY THE REMAINS OF 86 SUMMERS. BEFORE US GLOWED THE PROMISE OF NEW TRADITIONS AND BETTER TIMES.

If you enjoyed this book, please post a review
at your favorite online bookstore. Thank you.